18 Ways

GOD

Wins in

2018

BY:

Dr. Siéta Achampong

2017 sure has been a doozy of a year for so many. I have spoken to a myriad of my friends, colleagues, coworkers, associates and even some church members, and all have said the same thing; "I sure can't wait for 2017 to be over!" I have seen so many posts, quotes and memes on social media all wishing that 2017 would magically and quickly disappear and take out all of the junk and baggage that it brought with it. People have just been so bogged down by 2017!

The funny or the most peculiar thing about it, however, is when I questioned my friends and coworkers etc. about what made 2017 so horrible and troublesome, I seem to get the same resounding answer; "I don't know" they repeatedly say to me. "I just can't put my finger on what made 2017 one of the worst years of my life." I cannot judge them. I do not fault them at all, and I actually agree with them 100%. Just like so many, I walked in 2017 – no my mistake – I stormed in 2017, proudly proclaiming that this was my year! This was going to be the year of years; ultimate everything! This would be the year that I get my business started and booming; the year my book would be finished and published; the year that I would hit my swag in my career; the year when it all just honestly would come completely together. I even declared on social media that I was leaving 2016 behind, and although 2016 had been very good to me, I could only imagine what God had in store for His vessel in 2017. Greatness was coming. I was certain I was going to win. Well my my, my, my, my, was I wrong!

I hit a brick wall. Smack into it; dead-end sign with no way of making a U-turn to get back on the right track. I was stuck and felt paralyzed. No matter what I tried to do to motivate myself, nothing seemed to move me to work on, let alone accomplish, all of the goals I intended to master in 2017. I have always been a person that no matter what was happening to her or around her I would use that particular situation to motivate me to do better. When I became pregnant at the age of 14 and my family members discovered my hidden now public sin they would often ridicule me and my grandparents (they raised me) and declared over my life that I would amount to nothing. I had ruined my life. See, I did not always stay in a child's place, and I eavesdropped in on the adult conversations. I heard what they said about me, words those spiteful adults said about a child behind her back. Some, however, told me directly to my face that I would end up having multiple children before I reached the age of 20 and would be living on welfare for the rest of my life. I was destined to be a failure. I honestly cannot recall one positive conversation or words of encouragement from any of my close family members or from adults in my life at the time. Perhaps I blocked them all out, or reality, they simply did not occur. I cannot recall anyone saying to me that this was a time in my life that I could recover and learn from this experience. Yes, having a child at any age is a life altering experience and to have a child as a child would be challenging beyond measure; but success and making "it" was possible. No one said to me that you can graduate from high school and live an abundant life even as a teen parent.

I remember one night stretching across my grandparent's bed and having a conversation with my grandfather. He shook his head at me, as he often would, and said, "Now you are not going to graduate from high school." Confidently, I looked him square in the eyes, and I said, "Yes I will Pop! And not only will I graduate from high school but I will also graduate from college!" He did not look convinced at all, and my heart sank to my stomach but I was fueled to prove everyone who doubted me wrong. Our conversation catapulted me to want to make my grandfather proud of me and to prove to all of my haters that they would regret spewing the venom of life failure over me. And I did. Well, God did! Not only did my grandfather witness me walk across the high school graduation stage but he also witnessed me graduate with my Bachelor's degree. And although he was wheelchair bound, God saw fit for my grandfather to even witness my master's degree graduation ceremony. At the end of the ceremony, I walked over and hugged his neck, smiled and said, "See Pop, I told you I would graduate." And in his way, he cocked his head to the side and gave me a slight smile. I knew he was proud of me, and he did not have to utter one single word.

Negativity and obstacles fueled me. People telling me "you can't!" made me push harder, and I was more determined to prove "Yes, I can!" I was the insurmountable obstacle hurdler. Life continued to throw boulders and bricks smack dab in my face. Trial after trial I faced, and it was almost unreal – movie like. I myself could not believe the amount of hurt, pain, disappointment, and fearful experiences I encountered in my young life. It all felt unfair and time and time again I wanted to tell God that I had had enough! But no matter the circumstance, somehow, through God, I was victorious. I made it!

So, what makes this time so different? Why am I stuck and cannot move just one step forward? What has 2017 done to me to make me so jaded and powerless? That's how I feel - powerless. Had 2017 sucked my woman power completely out of me? Did 2017 erase the years of building up my strength to accomplish great things in spite of? That is what I did. I accomplished great things, the impossible things simply because I believed it was possible in spite of the odds against me. Had I finally reached a point in my life where "you can't" was now my reality? Where is God? Why couldn't I hear Him speak to me as He did all those years? Why was He not making a way as He had done in the past... for me? Why was God silent?

Reflection is deep. You know if you are truly honest with yourself and look yourself in the mirror and are willing to know that you and you alone are responsible for you; reflection is deep. I reflected and said girl if you do not stop and do what you have done all of your life, do what grandmother and pop pop taught you at an early age when you had no clue where your help was going to come from. PRAY and earnestly seek God. Shut out the noise of your everyday life and ask God to show you the way. So I did just that, and guess what ...He actually did it! My God again showed me the way and opened up my ears; He softened my hardened heart and decluttered my cloudy mind. I reflected. And then I prayed, and I pleaded with God to give me some insight and to make me see what I needed to see... see from Him and Him alone, see what He was requiring of me to move forward.

So it was not a complete surprise to me when a friend encouraged me to write 18 ways God Will Win in 2018. Although this was not what I thought I would write, yet God in His infinite wisdom knew I needed to write these words to not only encourage you but to work on me and to reassure myself to climb out of the sink hole of nothingness and darkness that surrounded me in 2017. Are you ready for a real change? Do you want more out of your life? Do you desire more for not only yourself, but for your family and friends? Are you ready for your blessings in order for you to be a blessing to others? Are you ready to WIN? Well, I know I sure am! I am ready for victorious living! Let's do this together. Take a walk with me as we throw out 2017 and keep it in our rear view mirrors and anticipate 2018 with great expectation.

God Wins... Don't Abandon Your Hopes & Dreams

Psalm 37:4 ESV Delight yourself in the Lord, and he will give you the desires of your heart.

As a young child, I would play school with my stuffed animals, cousins and neighborhood friends. I knew deep in my spirit that I was destined to be an educator. I was good at teaching people and getting them to listen to me even at a very young age. The younger kids in the neighborhood would do almost anything I told– I mean – asked them to do. Some called me bossy but I prefer to say I used assertive persuasion. I loved it! It gave me great joy to see a face light up because I was able to show someone something they had not previously known. It was amazing! So, needless to say I was beyond myself when I grew up, graduated from college, and landed my first teaching job almost immediately after graduation. Talk about God's favor! As the years moved on, I earned my master's degree and principal's certification and eventually became a principal, a career I absolutely love. And then God just showed all the way off and blessed me with my doctorate degree. Woo! Hoo! I had reached the pinnacle of education. So, what happens now? Is this the end of all of my dreams and goals? Is this it?

Once again I was flat– stale. Coming down off of the high of hearing people say Dr. before my name, I found myself looking around and asking is this all? I should be over the moon and filled off of all I had accomplished, right? so why was I feeling like I needed more? One late evening this school year I was having a conversation with one of my teachers and we laughed about our younger selves and all the things we said we were going to do and be when we got older. She shared her dreams of becoming a famous movie star and I replied with my dream of being a published author and motivational speaker. After we shared some more laughter and crazy stories she left for the evening. Driving home, I couldn't help but think if part of the reason why I was feeling half-full was because I had totally abandoned my other childhood dreams. And why had I done so; what were my reasons? Well I had plenty: my children and family, my demanding career, my church commitments and the list could go on and on. Excuses. Not real reasons for me to have let my other dreams dissipate.

Remember those times as a child when you felt you could accomplish anything? Dreams and goals had no limits. In fact, you envisioned exactly what color your princess dress would be as you danced your first dance with your prince. You would wear your favorite super hero cape as you soared around saving the world in your mind. Your dreams and goals were real. No one and nothing could tell you otherwise. So, let me ask you; how does your tiara fit?

Too often we grow up and become adults and we completely forget about our childhood goals, hopes, and dreams. We sweep them into a corner or bury them under a rug and forget them. Life becomes mundane and drab. Then one day we go to move and uncover what we tried to forget and we wonder why we hid them in the first place. Why did we not go after what we wanted?

God has a way of bringing things back full circle and to our remembrance for a reason and at just the right time. Could 2018 be the year when you nostalgically dream and hope and work on those goals you always wanted to accomplish? Let God win in your life by understanding that if we delight ourselves in the Lord, he will give us the desires of our hearts (Psalm 37:4). Do not be afraid to dream as you did as a little child – colorful and bold!

God Wins...

Forgive So You Can Heal

Bear with each other and forgive one another if any of you has a grievance against someone. Forgive as the Lord forgave you." <u>Colossians 3:13</u>

She left us...she died and left us without a mother. And I was angry. How dare she choose alcohol and drugs over her two beautiful daughters? Selfish woman! Didn't she realize by dying she would miss graduations, beautiful wedding dresses and weddings, births and cake and ice cream – who will eat the cake and ice cream? Our children will never get the opportunity to share one of Little Grandmom's infamous hugs that literally took your breath away. They will never know her; she will not even be a thought in their minds. Resentful.

I refused to cry at her funeral. I told her to her face that if she died I would not cry at her funeral. I was a woman of my word. Only 17 years old when my mother died and left me motherless with a baby and no way of knowing what would be next in my life. I would allow not one tear to slip from my eyes. She did this hateful thing to herself and to us. How dare she leave me! Resentful.

Life moved on for me and my sister after my mother died, and we both defied the societal odds. Truth is I was maturing, moving and growing in multiple arenas of my life with the exception of this one. I had mommy issues and didn't even know about. A mother's love is like no other love. I never felt without a shadow of doubt that my mother truly loved me. In my heart and mind I felt there was no way she loved me – how could someone choose a crack pipe over her very own daughters? Abandoned, scared, and confused – mommy issues for sure. "You are going to end up just like your mother." Those are the words directed at me that flowed so effortlessly out of the mouths of the loving family members after her death. "No I will not!" I absolutely declared and wanting so desperately to not become like my mother, I discovered a way to neutralize my mommy issues and completely block out the hurt. It worked too! For years of my life I was able to move forward in life – it worked! And then once again life issues and life reality hit, and I could no longer hold the defense wall up – it shattered all around me and I was forced to face my mommy issues.

The truth of the matter is I was in a fight with someone who could not or no longer defend herself. But I wanted to fight – an argument; or at least a heated discussion as to why she chose this lifestyle over her family. That was not going to happen – she was dead. At 17, still a child, I watched the drugs and alcohol my mother abused finally KO her permanently. I had to realize prior to her death my mother could barely utter her own name let alone provide me an explanation as to why she could not resist these urges and just had to succumb. And when she was herself and could explain I was just not old enough. Mothers do not tell their children those types of things. Good mothers don't share the pain and the hurt and the loneliness and the unthinkable forced forgiven with their children. They just do not. For years I resented her because I could not understand her "why". Mommy issues caught up to me and once again paused my momentum. I knew I had to stop fighting with the air – with something- I mean someone -who no longer existed. My arms were growing tired and weak from throwing punches that landed nowhere.

I had to forgive her. I often tell people that you should not punish kids for adult mistakes; well in this particular case I told myself you can no longer punish yourself for your mother's mistakes. Forgive her for she knows not what she has done. As a mature adult now with lots of life baggage and experience, I understand my mother's living reality. Whatever hurt her in her young life propelled her in a downward spiral. No one probably ever held her hand and gave her hope or provided her with another way out; so she did what made her feel good even if the feeling was temporary. She could not find her way out. She was completely shattered and broken. Broken people cannot demonstrate their love to others no matter how hard they try. She loved me - yes she did - her infamous hugs told me so! And I had to remind myself of that even though most of my life my mother's struggle overshadowed my mother's love. So, I forgive her for dying. God knew best that she needed to be rescued from her tormented life and now she has finally found the peace and joy that surpasses all understanding. It is my time to find joy. I forgive my mother and now I can heal.

In 2018, God will win in our lives through sincere forgiveness and healing. Day after day we sin and fall short of his glory. Yet God in His way, when we repent and genuinely seek His forgiveness, He forgives us and wipes our slates clean. We, in return, must do the same for others; even those who cannot or will not ask for forgiveness. Bear with each other and forgive one another if any of you has a grievance against someone. Forgive as the Lord forgave you; and watch God Win in your life.

God
Wins...
Work for the Lord

Whatever you do, work at it with all of your heart, as working for the Lord, not for men.
Colossians 3:23

I think I might be in the minority when I say that I honestly enjoy going to work every day. Although at times this job is stressful and I question if I am actually making a difference, I know deep down inside I could not imagine working or doing anything else at this time in my life. Now, look, it was not always easy street. There was a time in my career when I worked in a very toxic and draining work environment. It was tormenting. Day after day you never knew what to expect from the evil spirits that were in charge. One minute they would smile in your face and praise you for your good work, and the next second you were packing your office up – fired just like that. Crazy for sure. I knew things were out of control when grown men would come in my office and cry like they were children again, abused by the powers that be and afraid of what might come next. My health was impacted by the stress we all were under and endured. The roller coaster ride made us all violently ill. We could not take it any longer, and the majority of us began to apply for other positions. I watch some of my dear friends leave for other jobs and my heart would sink time and time again because God had not quite opened a door for me. I was stuck in the living nightmare.

I was approached at church during this time to take a stewardship class. I agreed and went into the class with the mindset that I would learn how to better handle my finances according to God's word. And I did, but the good Lord had something greater in store for me. Not only did I learn about my finances but I also learned the importance of working for the Lord and not for man. I was so wrapped up and worried about the limitless power of my overseers that I took my eyes and mind off of the only one who holds all power! So, I reset my thinking and began faithfully praying and listening to only spirit filling music as it softly played through my laptop during the day. Doors of new opportunities continued to close in my face. But I stayed still and reminded myself again and again that my work was for the Lord. I could literally feel God carrying me through this storm. Finally God opened up my door of hope, and I glided out of that place with a smile knowing God had won that battle in my favor.

My dear girlfriend still worked there and stayed faithfully for many years after my departure. For the most part, things were just fine for her; new management had taken over and she was working and changing lives. Nothing major – right. Wrong! 2017 strikes again. Just like that she went from being an exemplary worker to a piece of trash that must be immediately discarded. She had no clue this was coming. There was no sign that indicated to her the road was permanently closed ahead and she needed to exit expeditiously for her own safety. The new work master had a conniving plan that was for his career benefit, but to the detriment of my good friend. She was devastated when the word came down that it was her time to leave the place she loved and not by her own choice.

She called me. I almost could not make out that it was she even though the caller ID on my cell scrolled her name. "What's wrong?" I said with a worried trembling voice. I could not understand what she was trying to tell me. "I can't understand you sis...why are you crying?" I said. She paused and I could tell she was trying desperately to gain her composure. Finally a breath, a pause, and then she was able to tell me the knife-stabbing news. I was in shock. How was this possible? She was amazing at what she did. Never received a write-up; major complaint; everybody absolutely adored her; she was the bomb.com as the kids used to say. How in the world was she let go just like that?

And she asked the very same questions. But so it was. This was her truth and her reality. She would not wake up and realize it was all a dream – no she was living her nightmare. Hit by the reality that human beings are filthy, my girlfriend was forced to deal with how the sins of others ripple and destroy an entire community. Oh, she was hurt. I could feel the pain she carried deep each and every time we spoke. Disbelief. At times pure agony would rumble up from the pit of her stomach and out of her mouth and she would cry out – "Why me!" It was devastating to watch my strong sister melt like a snowman on a mild winter day. She was destroyed.

God spoke and told me to remind her of my very own experience. And I did just that. I told my Sis that God gives and God taketh away. We do our work to please God and not man and all she had to remember was that no weapon formed to destroy her professional career would ever prosper. We work for the Lord. Many times we do not listen, and we fail to read the tea leaves on the trees. Often God gives us warning signs that danger lies ahead, but we can do all things by myself humans miss the flashing warning lights, and signs and we fail to make the needed exit change. So at times God has to force us to move. My girlfriend and I talked and prayed and came to the conclusion that If God decided He wanted us to physically change our work environment, who were we to argue and say "Naw, God I am alright. I prefer to stay right where I am – I am comfortable- thank you." Yeah right! What a joke. God is omniscient; He knows all things and that includes what is best for us even in the work world.

So, God gives and God takes away as He sees fit. Slowly my girlfriend began to live this truth. She started a brand new position in a brand new place and never missed a beat. God is working on her heart and helping her see the greater good in this life circumstance. The sun is starting to shine more days than not in her life again. God is reminding her daily through her new work experiences that He ultimately wins and has the final say.

As you begin this transition into 2018, how will God Win in your professional and work career? Perhaps you work in an unfulfilling job, and you ache at the thought of going to work every day. Or, by chance, you are like me and you delight in your job and really do not see the need for change. No matter what your work situation or circumstances are, God Wins in 2018 when we approach each work day and experience remembering whatever we do work at it with all of our heart, as working for the Lord, not for man.

God
Wins...
My Protector

But the Lord is faithful, and he will strengthen you and protect you from the evil one. **2 Thessalonians 3:3**

Fear has paralyzed me. Outside I am this tough shell that many people rarely see break; but inside fear swirls around in me paralyzing me from living. I am so petrified that I cannot even walk my dog in the dark. I AM AFRAID. Whew, that felt good to verbalize. He made me afraid to live again. He? Who is he? The man who thought it not robbery to rob me by knife point a few years ago.

It was a regular morning, and I was following my regular routine. I had been warned by my police friends and family to change up my routine because I had been experiencing some issues with a former employee. Unfortunately, this young man violated a policy and was let go. He was infuriated and began to stalk and harass me. I never knew what to expect or when he would just pop up. This went on for almost two years. So, I was advised to change up my schedule. I did not. Popop used to say "A hard head leads to a soft behind." This was true to me. On this morning I followed my normal routine, left the house at 4:45 am, and drove singing praises to the Lord, and stopped at the Dunkin Donuts to grab my morning coffee. I felt good, and it was going to be a great day. I whipped my car into my normal parking space. I glanced up and noticed a man standing by the front door with his hood up. He seemed to have nodded his head as if to say "yep this is the one." I hesitated. Something in my spirit gave me pause. I thought for a second and then said to myself with all of these bright lights and this major busy street, he would not dare do anything to me – too many witnesses. Wrong again! I got out of my car and quickly walked past the hooded stranger and into the store. I was a regular, and the workers knew me and my order well. My coffee was already prepared, and the young lady handed me my cup and we both said, "Have a good day!" Out the door I dashed.

I felt him behind me so I turned, and we were face to face. Startled, I queried, "What do you need sir?" "Give me you wallet!" he sternly told me in his broken English. "Excuse me?" I asked. I was confused. What was happening here? "Give me you wallet!" he said again, this time yanking on my right arm trying to take my purse off of my shoulder and pushing me backwards. My coffee dropped to the ground. I look down and realized the knife pushed up against my chest. Peddling backwards, my shoes fall off. I thought, "ok, the knife isn't that big try to take him. No! What if he stabs you? What about your children? Change in plans – give him the purse." So I did. I shoved my purse towards him and started to yell Help! Help! Help! as loud as I possibly could. Surely someone inside would hear me and run out and save me from this unthinkable ordeal. The hooded stranger ran off toward the car he had parked on the side. I sprinted back into the store yelling "Help me! Please help me! That man just took my purse!" The workers looked perplexed – obviously they had not heard or seen anything. There was a man standing in line and he recognized what I was saying and turned with me to run back out of the store. I pointed to the left to my assailant; he was still sitting in his car rummaging through my purse. "There he is!" The good Samaritan took one step forward, and then he paused, turned and directed the store manager to call the police. The hooded stranger sped off with my purse – with all I had including my flash drive with my only electronic copy of my dissertation.

I sank. There goes it all. All of my hard work down the drain. Furious and shaking my voice, trembling, I asked to use someone's cell phone to call my husband to inform him of my new tragedy and for him to bring the extra keys to the car. I was in total shock. Me. This happened to me. The police arrived and took my statement. They released a picture of the hooded assailant as captured off of store video. However, there were no real leads, no breaking news; my purse was never found, and neither of my cell phones (work and personal) were turned back on again to be traced. He was never apprehended.

Cold case. He not only had my personal belongings, but he also now had control over me.

"PTSD." That's what you have" – my psychologist friend bluntly told me. "You need to go to counseling." I agreed, but a series of unfortunate events and uncomfortable instances trying to schedule my first counseling session prevented me from following this directive. Instead I decided to just move forward on my own. Well, that is just not working out. I am still afraid. My heart pounds – rapidly races and sweat drips down my forehead. I shake and immediately my eyes see him and that unforgettable moment when the thought of going to that particular Dunkin Donuts hits my mind, or when I drive by. I jump when people unexpectedly approach me from behind. My mind tells me that he could be anywhere; lurking, watching my every move and waiting to attack me again. What if he was not finished? What if this time he physically hurts me? PTSD. Traumatized. Yep. This unbreakable, solid rock of a woman who has endured, survived and been victorious over relationship domestic violence; abandonment; and assault could not recover from the hooded stranger.

I am afraid. But I trust God. In 2018 I am admitting to the Lord that I will truly trust Him as my protector in good times and bad times. I recognized that although this happened to me -yes it happened to me- I am still here to share my testimony. God protected me even during those terrifying minutes that felt like eternity. God was there. He blocked him from stabbing me and he entered my mind to change the thoughts to fight back to spare my life. God knew I would not win. Material things have all been replaced and I was able to finish my dissertation and graduate on time. Most importantly I am still here for my family. God is faithful.

God Wins in 2018 because He is our protector. I must reclaim my life. He can no longer have control. I want to fully live and enjoy without worry. And in 2018 I proclaim that I will. What has a stronghold on you and has you paralyzed with fear? What is preventing you to live your best life? Are you suffering from PTSD, and you have no idea how you will move ahead? Be encouraged because the Lord our God is faithful, and he will strengthen you and protect you from the evil one. All you have to do is believe. God is our Protector.

God
Wins...
Dumb the Tea

Let no unwholesome word proceed from your mouth, but only such a word as is good for edification according to the need of the moment, so that it will give grace to those who hear.
Ephesians 4:29

You know what is truly irking my spirit in 2017? Women degrading and putting down other women. It is just disrespectful, and it is getting us absolutely nowhere. I feel like once upon a time women supported one another. When something great happened to a woman she would share her news, and her sister friend would be just as proud and elated for her as if it were herself. Ha! Gone are the days. I blame ratchet reality television and social media. Yup. They are the culprits. The reason why what we used to say in the dark and behind a fellow sisters' back is now on public display for all to like, comment, and share. We are tearing each other down in public with no shame and as if we all are living in glass houses. We are something else.

Women have an opinion and commentary on everything. I read my social media comments at times, and what I read never ceases to amaze me.

"Honey, if that were me I would have left him. How dare he have those babies and still think he is going to stay married to me?"

"She's a fool! Not me!"

"Hum! She thinks she's all that because she got a little education."

"She still ain't nothing even if she does have a doctorate degree."

"Look at her with those run down shoes and cheap dress. I thought she said she had money?"

"I wouldn't be caught dead in that outfit."

"Her children are disrespectful and need discipline. Wouldn't be my kids."

"Those aren't even his kids."

"If she don't go somewhere with those demon eyebrows!"

"Her weave is past due!"

"Why she so petty tho'?"

And the negative and judgmental comments go on and on. Way to go women! We sure have a way of speaking life!

What makes matters worse to me is the lack of woman respect that is demonstrated in the workplace. It is hard enough for a woman to rise to the top to have a seat and be offered a plate at the table; and to command the same respect our male counterparts naturally receive. We must also defend ourselves against our workplace women. We have to fight and deal with the woman-bullying and secret hate from our female colleagues. It's exhausting! Instead of encouragement, women exercise their right to destroy. We sneak behind backs and come up with elaborate stories and schemes to eliminate our perceived competition. We gossip, tell lies, and ruin reputations without hesitation, thought, or care. And don't let me forget the lack of positive women mentors in the professional arena. As soon as she makes it to the top, she forgets to reach back to mold, shape, assist and help the next sister reach her potential. I have encountered so many selfish women leaders caught up in their own personal success world they become the worst examples to follow. Sad.

Women, we must admit- we are brutal and show no mercy. We demonize a woman for staying with her husband when he has been unfaithful. We laugh and criticize a woman for being overweight and tell a woman who is thin to eat more chicken. We are a mess! Any opportunity we get we are ready and willing to make, pour, sip, and spill the tea. And why not- right? What does it matter anyway? Society has made it okay for us to belittle and destroy through our gossiping tongues.

The word of God teaches death and life are in the power of the tongue. Therefore, what we say to and about one another can make the literal difference between life and death. Absolutely so. Our young growing and budding women are watching our every move and hanging on to our every word. They see and hear everything we are doing to murder the spirit of another woman. I sit back and listen to some of my high school students and shake my head in amazement at times at the things they tell me they hear come out the mouths of their very own mothers, women who are charged to set the ultimate positive example for their children.

Yes, we are charged to set the positive example, ladies, and we must! We must guard our lips and end our gossiping. Let us take up the cause and learn how to pour out and speak life. Let no unwholesome word proceed form our mouths, but only such a word as is good for edification according to the need of the moment, so that it will give grace to those who hear. Walk into 2018 allowing God to win by permanently dumping out the negative tea. Indulge in water instead, the Living water; you'll be heathier and wiser.

God
Wins...
Lead with Love

Husbands, love your wives, just as Christ loved the church and gave himself up for her.
Ephesians 5:25

Men you are not off the hook! No siree Bob! You all definitely have some things to work on and leave behind in 2017. Now, I am not a man, and I am not going to begin to pretend that I absolutely understand a man's world. However, I spend time around men at work, church, home, volunteer opportunities, you name it, and I observe and take notes. But what perhaps gives me a deeper insight into you, man, is that I spend the most time with fiancée's, wives, mothers, sisters, girlfriends and even side-chicks. And they share with me a lot, and to be honest sometimes, a little too much. But I listen, and I advise when it is appropriate. In addition, I reflect and pay attention to my own personal experiences with men. I have come to one major conclusion – men it is time to let go of childish ways and lead and love as Christ.

Men you have been charged with the ultimate responsibility to lead. Some of you have a clear, biblical understanding of what it means to lead while others... well let's just say you are still walking around in the wilderness. Some men believe leading means dictating while they sit on his throne and their wife and children serve him and obey his every command. Some men feel it is the woman's responsibility to bring home the bacon, fry it up, and serve it too; all the while they sit and watch television all day long. One man told me that a woman must learn how to stay in her place and that if I were his wife he never would have allowed me to go back to school. Well, I kindly replied to him that is why I wasn't his wife and perhaps the reason he doesn't have one now. Interesting isn't it?

Too many men are strutting around trying to prove and show to everyone that they are the M-A-A-A-A-N doing all sorts of this and that to boost their self-esteem and confidence and engaging in intimate, and at times inappropriate, relationships with multiple women at the same time; lying to and convincing their wives or significant others that they must have had that STD before they got together. He did not give her a thing, even though both he and she know she's been with no one else. Or casually sliding into another woman's DM because she says just the right thing that makes him feel good. Buying expensive toys and items and destroying the household budget and then demanding she fix his money issues. Sitting back and kicking his feet up while his wife works all day, comes home and cooks, helps the kids with homework, takes them to their evening extracurricular activities, washes and folds a load of laundry, goes to bed without a kiss or a thank you, and wakes up the next morning to do it all over again. Working long hours weekdays and weekends because it gives him that satisfaction he thirst, but he never takes the time to water the plants at home and his wife and children are all dried up.

Now, do not get me wrong, my dear men out there; it is so important that we women give you what you need and love you according to your love language. We must take intentional time to say and do things to reaffirm you as the man... our man. However, men, I listen to these women, and some are loving you with all they have, yet their best is not even close to being good enough. Men, it is time for you to recognize you have baggage as well that you need to unload so that you can lead with love. It is not her fault you never knew your daddy, and your mother hated looking at you because you reminded her so much of "that deadbeat man." The woman in your life is not responsible for the fact you never had a positive role model to follow and to show you what a committed and loving relationship should look like and function. Stop secretly resenting her because of your past junk you do not want to face; deal with it; give to God, and forgive. It is not her fault.

She needs your unconditional love, and you must find a way to work through your issues in order to provide what you have been charged to give. She is deeply hurting and is in desperate need for her man to help her recover and heal. Treat her like the queen she is, and she will have no problem at all giving you your kingly crown. Men allow God to win in 2018 by putting away childish games and ways and lead with love as Christ loved the church and gave himself up for her. Love her as you love your own bodies because he who loves her, loves himself.

God Wins... Walk Away from Toxic Relationships

Leave the presence of a fool, Or you will not discern words of knowledge. Proverbs 14:7

2017 has shined a bright spotlight of reality directly in my face when it comes to relationships. Not my romantic marriage relationship per se, but friendships and freindlikeships (yes I made that word up) type of relationships. A light so bright I developed a migraine, stressing over what exactly I did wrong to cause all of this mess and attention? What happened that disturbed the peace and awakened the sleeping dead? How can I fix this? What a whirlwind of emotions I tell ya for sure.

I am not afraid to admit that I have a very strong personality. I can dominate a conversation, take over a meeting, change the direction and minds of the masses, and make insecure people wish I had never shown up. Some might feel at times I can be a little scary and mean, but I simply cannot tolerate certain things done in certain ways, especially if they hurt other people. Tough. I can be tough to handle at times. Shoot... sometimes I can't even deal with my own self. But I know my issues and faults, and I honesty seek God and work on them daily – what about you? Looking in my reflection mirror, I know I can be a lot to handle, but I also know that when it comes to relationship, you won't find a more loyal friend.

Due to my life history experiences and personality, I am very particular about who I let into my life. So if you make it into my inner circle – you have arrived! No seriously, I am guarded for many reasons, so I treasure the friends and relationships I form. In the past if someone hurt me or betrayed me, I put up my wall and pretended that he/she no longer existed, and I moved on with my life. Dead to me. It was easy for me to do because it was the same tactic I used to protect myself from the crazy relationship I had with my mother. It worked for me. Of course until this year.

See, I found out the hard way that when you spend years in a relationship with someone and you go through the ups and downs and the truly good times and what-the-heck-were-we-thinking times; it is not so easy to pronounce the benediction over the relationship and bounce. As we grow and mature, we learn people are not that dispensable, and you cannot always walk away – even when they hurt you so badly you feel as if you were going to truly die. Some relationships are worth fighting for while others have reached such a high level of toxicity, you begin to disintegrate from the side effects and need to let them go.

You all know those toxic people who claim they are your "true" friends. Yes, the ones who only call you when they have an issue or concern for you to fix. But when you call with your problem they always say they are busy and will call you right back. Well, two weeks later when you hear from them again, you are reaching into your wallet to get out the $20 they want to borrow right quick. The one who dumps, dumps, dumps but never comes back around to pick up her trash. They are negative all the time and expect you to jump on their bandwagon of pessimism, and when you do not, you are not being a good friend. In their eyes you are the one who needs to change. Toxic. Yes, the so called friend who on the surface appears to be happy about your success, but you catch them out the corner of your eye rolling their eyes with an attitude during your celebration party.

Toxic friends are violators of the heart. This year has taught me that I must learn how to differentiate between relationships that are worth fighting for and relationships that need to be discarded liked a bad habit. Allowing the so-called friends who do nothing to edify me but only suck the life out of me has to end not now but right now. I can no longer shoulder the toxic burdens they bring into my life time and time again.

How about you? Have you been drained by a toxic relationship in 2017? Did you sit back and ponder if you were going crazy, or was something completely upside down when it came to some or your relationships? Trust me, you are not imagining things at all, and you must act quickly because if you stay, you limit your ability to personally grow, serve, and mentor others. Toxic friends are fools, and until they are honest with themselves, they will never be able to change.

God wins in 2018 when we learn to distinguish between healthy relationships and relationships that stink like trash. Then we must let go of the foul smelling toxic relationships. Leave the presence of the foolish friend so that you can be able to discern the words of knowledge and be a blessing to yourself and others.

God Wins...
Get Rid of the Masks

You can't keep your true self hidden forever; before long you'll be exposed. You can't hide behind a religious mask forever; sooner or later the mask will slip and your true face will be known. Luke 12:2

Several years ago while exercising at aqua aerobics, I listened to a girlfriend and workout partner tell me about her co-worker who was struggling with depression. She told me how this co-worker tried medicine and counseling, but neither seemed to be easing the co-worker's depressed state. Depression was destroying this co-worker's everyday life. I was in a good place in my life at the time and was really confident in my walk with Christ; arrogantly, I replied to my girlfriend, "I don't believe in depression. If people are depressed it is because they lack faith in God." I then boldly declared, "Your co-worker isn't seeing any progress you say? That's because he hasn't really tried God." I was confident my words were the absolute truth, and I just knew that if my friend would share my advice, her co-worker would be healed and delivered! My friend just gave me her side-eye as if to say, "oh you foolish woman." I noticed; I didn't care; I was right! So, I just kept on wading through the pool and changed the subject of our conversation.

You know God has a way of teaching you lessons even when you thought you had already passed the class. Not too long after this exchange in the water, I started experiencing health issues. Doctor visit after doctor visit; emergency room trip one after the other; pain that could not be explained. Exhausted and tired, I began to tunnel down a dark path. Barely holding on to hope, I believe the tipping point for me was when my husband and I miscarried for the second time. We had been trying for a while and were in a research study. The study ended, and we were still not pregnant so we thought well, once again – nothing. So we went on with our lives. A month and half to two months later, I was at work. It was a crazy and hectic day: I did not even get the chance to use the restroom all day. Finally, no longer able to hold, it I hurried into the ladies' restroom. Something was not right. I composed myself; took a deep breath and walked back out towards my office. I could feel blood streaming down my legs. I went to my office and phoned my husband telling him one of two things was happening: I was either having another miscarriage or I was hemorrhaging. Either way I was on my way to the hospital. Hanging up the phone, I walked out and explained to one of my staff members that I had an emergency and needed to go to the ER immediately. He called another staff member, and she came to my office full of concern. I told her what I thought was happening and that I was driving myself to the hospital. Knowing that I would not allow it to be any other way, she informed me she would follow me there in her car to ensure I got their safely. My male staff member picked up on our conversation and grabbed a large black trash bag –"here," he said use this in your car to sit on."

We made it to the hospital and seeing all of the blood everywhere, they took me back right away. After a few tests and an ultrasound my fear was confirmed. The doctor came in and bluntly told me and my husband, who arrived just in time, "you miscarried." "You didn't know you were pregnant?" was the question I kept getting at the hospital and even when I returned home -No; I did not. The accusatory tone in which the question was posed made me feel that others blamed me for the death of the baby. And I guess I blamed myself as well. How did I not know? If I would have known, I would have been taking better care of myself and perhaps this baby would have been born full term. Was this my fault? Was I paying for my sins of my past? This miscarriage was different. It was painful physically and mentally. Was God sending me a message?

Depression introduced himself to me. He met me at the front door of my mind and my heart. All I wanted to do was sleep. I had no desire to do much of anything at all; including going to church. Everything was dark. I had no joy doing anything. You know when you go to the doctor, and the nurse or doctor asks if you have been feeling down or thought about hurting yourself in the past two weeks? Well, my doctor asked me, and with my eyes filled with tears, I clenched my teeth to stop them from falling, looked her square in the eye, and painfully said "no." I was lying, and she knew it. But of course I had to keep my mask on tight and not reveal to anyone, not even my doctor, that there was a battle – a brutal war of good versus evil inside my body, and evil was winning. I had to keep up my front by performing my daily activities struggling through them in my mind but putting on an Oscar winning performance outwardly so no one could make me out.

I remember driving to a speaking engagement, and the dark thoughts started creeping in my mind. I was so down and low I absolutely did not know what to do. I was mentally sick and now physically weak. I didn't even have the strength to pray and call on the Lord for help. Crossing over a bridge, the dark thoughts spoke, "do it now!" It will be quick, easy, and you won't feel a thing. Do it now. End your suffering." I contemplated. I could do this now, and all the pain I was suffering would be over. Then a picture of my two beautiful daughters flashed before my eyes. I smiled and shook my head. I looked up with tears streaming down my face – praise God, I was over the bridge. I made it to my speaking engagement, spoke to the crowd about life and living your best life; and took another route back home. Sitting in my garage, I cried out loud "Lord, please help me! I surrender!"

Still filled with too much pride and afraid that people would judge me if I took my mask off and revealed who I really was and what I was dealing with, I sought the counsel of a friend who is a professional counselor. Timid and afraid that even she would judge what I was hiding under my mask, I tip-toed around until she finally said, "until you are real with yourself you will never heal and get back to the person who you really are." She was spot on. So, I slowly took it off – my mask of perfection and unlimited strength. I finally admitted I was depressed, and then I could take the necessary steps towards healing and recovery.

Depression is real. Is a stronghold like no other, and many are suffering from its grip. So many of us wear masks, desperately trying to hide and cover up our hurts, battles, scars, damage, and the list goes on and on. Whether it is depression, addiction, insecurity, loneliness, or just plain old hurt from this tumultuous life we are all living– we all wear masks in an attempt to hide what we are honestly going through in our lives; afraid that the world will judge us, look down on us. It is time we ripped off our masks and hand them over to the only One who is capable.

There are dangers when we continue to wear our mask; we allow evil to take up residence, and we cannot be true witnesses to those who need it most. We can no longer keep our true selves and what we are facing hidden forever; before we know it we will be exposed; we cannot hide behind a religious mask forever; sooner or later the mask will slip and our true face will be known. Let God Win in 2018 by getting rid of the mask of lies you wear day after day. Remove the mask so that you will win.

God
Wins...
You Are Enough

For we are God's handiwork, created in Christ Jesus to do good works, which God prepared in advance for us to do. Ephesians 2:10

"I am strong. I am powerful. I am beautiful." These words are the mantra one of the characters in a popular 2017 woman's movie repeated to herself. These nine words pierced me like a sword as soon as she said them. I desperately needed to hear them. I needed to be reminded that I am strong. I am powerful. And I am beautiful. God has done a great work in me. I needed to walk in his way and the path he had created for me. No questions asked and no looking back. I am enough.

Insecurities have always lingered in my spirit. Having a baby at an early age, I never had the best body and was self-conscious particularly about my stretch marked, scarred stomach. The cystic acne on my face and the lasting blemishes from family members popping my pimples when I was young convinced me I was not beautiful. In addition, no one had ever said directly to me "hey you are beautiful," hence one of the reasons I purposefully tell my daughters and my female students they are beautiful every chance I get. I was not even pretty. Words matter and words cut deep. Somewhere in my mid-twenties, I finally reached a point in my life when I realized that I was beautiful even if no one ever verbalized the words to me. I started to act and carry myself accordingly with confidence and owned every room I walked into. I knew I was strong. I was powerful, and, finally, I believed I was beautiful.

Life hits again and various negative life experiences and people started chipping away at my confidence. Suddenly, I found myself staring right back into the mirror of doubt. I started questioning my ability to do my job, to hold certain positions in my service organization. I started wondering if I really honestly belonged. I started to think these people are out of my league and I do not know if I can hang with them. They are all more accomplished than I am. I feel inferior. How did I get here? Why am I second guessing myself? What happened?

Do not sit there reading this with your high and mighty attitude because you and I both know you have asked yourself the same questions and felt insecure one point and time during your life. Remember now? I thought you would. Yes remember that time they passed you up for that promotion you knew you were more qualified for than the other candidate that got it instead of you? Remember when you overheard them talking about you behind your back and then came back and told you a completely different story? Remember that time they said you were just not the right person and if only your hair was longer, or you lost 10 more pounds, or if you had an 8 pack instead of 6 pack you would be the perfect person? Or maybe you remember when he or she left you for that other individual, and you asked yourself repeatedly what do they have that I do not? Yes, you remember. Insecurities.

Insecurities kill dreams and lives. Insecurities lead us down paths that God never intended for us to follow. We were all created for greatness because we were created by the ultimate Greatness – God. We cannot allow the perspectives of our society to continue to place boundaries around us – trapping us. We have to understand and firmly be committed to the notion that what God has for me, well, it is for me, and what God has for you, well, you know the rest.

You are enough. To be honest, 2017 and all of its drama made me feel that I was not enough for anything. I failed myself because I began to accept, as true, that there was a strong possibility I really did not have what it took to get the jobs done; I could not measure up. You are enough. Is what I told myself and what I am now preaching to you! You are enough! Believe it and go for it! It is your time. No matter what the "they's" of the world have to say or even think about you. If God says it is so, then it is so, and it is finished.

God wins in 2018 by reminding us that we are enough because we are His. For we are God's handiwork, created in Christ Jesus to do good works, which He prepared in advance for us to do." Will you believe and trust his word and direction and leave the insecurities at his feet? He can handle them – that is a fact!

God
Wins... Money Matters

Look at the birds of the air; they do not sow or reap or store away in barns, and yet your heavenly Father feeds them. Are you not much more valuable than they? Matthew 6:26

I could not help but to tear up as I listened to a gentleman share with me how, as a man, he feels like he has completely failed his family. He described to me the financial burdens and hardships that rocked his household this year and how he tried everything he could to manage the shake up, but to date he has not been successful. "I have failed my family," he said. "I am the man, and I am supposed to be able to provide for my family. All I want to is to be able to provide." He dropped his head in his hands and sighed deeply. My heart broke. I could feel his agony and worry. I could relate.

This year has been a financial disaster not only for this man and his family, but also for so many others I encountered as well as my own family. Businesses have failed. Bankruptcies have been filed and homes foreclosed. In my household, we had two graduate from college at the same time (that was not the plan by the way). Now the education bills are due, and we are not as prepared to pay them as we thought we were. Financially things started to fall apart for us in 2017, and we found ourselves in a very uncomfortable place. Fear and anxiety set in for me as I stressed over our money dilemma. See, this is why I hate money; all it does is cause problems! I now know why it is often quoted: "mo' money, mo' problems.' We sure are faced with problems, and mo' money is not in sight.

Do you know that money is mentioned in the Bible more than 800 times? Money matters and is a necessity for our everyday living here on this earth. Money in and of itself are not bad; yet the desire to gain money unethically or to worship money is a sin. We find ourselves in a little bit of a money situation, and the first thing we often do is wonder how we can get rich quick. We come up with some scheme or plan that will certainly eliminate our financial burdens. We take matters into our own hands. Then we have the nerve to get angry and upset when the plot fails, and we end up worse off financially then when we first started.

People are always discussing money and finances. Money is always on our minds. We worry about our next minute and how we are going to make a way out of no way. And therein lies our problem. WE want to make a way. We stress over money and provision as if we really have control. We do not. God is in control yesterday, today and tomorrow over everything including our bank accounts.

My dear brother and sister, I know you are financially strapped and in desperate need of relief. You do not see the sun on the horizon. It has been an entire year of money mess, and you see no way out. All of your bills are past due, and your money is low or even nonexistent. You are completely over your head. I know. I understand. But I challenge you to take your eyes off of your money problems and fix them on the Problem Solver. God will provide.

God wins in 2018 when we seek Him earnestly and give him total control over the one thing we often do not want anyone else on this earth to control or even know about – our money. I know your financial forecast looks bleak, but God says to "look at the birds in the air; they do not sow or reap or store away in barns, and yet your heavenly Father feeds them. Are you not much more valuable than they?" Money matters – yes even to God. He will win over you finances too!

God Wins...
Be Content

"Not that I am speaking of being in need, for I have learned in whatever situation I am to be content." Philippians4:11

Never satisfied! We are never, ever satisfied. We constantly thirst and yearn for more. Seeking and searching for more of what we think will make us complete. We tell ourselves, "if I only had this one more thing I would be just fine." We desire a more luxurious car, a bigger house, more money and status, someone else's perceived better life, and even their relationships and boo thangs. Honey, we aren't simply attempting to keep up with the Jones' but the Smith's and the Jackson's. And now with social media and the almost direct contact with celebrities, we are also trying to hang with Bruno and Beyoncé. Crazy right? Society has created this secret competition we are in with one another, and we all fall right into the trap. We want and must have more!

I was eavesdropping, I mean, I overheard a conversation between two women while I was waiting to pick up my order in the local deli. "Girl, I saw that on Instagram, and I am going to get it." The one woman boasted. "Just wait until I get my income tax check, and I am going to hit up my sister." "That's right girl!" The other woman replied. "You cannot let them out do you!" I could not help but to wonder what "it" was, but I knew whatever "it" was, she did not have "it" and wanted it badly. However, based on her own words, she really did not have the means to get "it." But it was clear not having the means was not going to stop her, and "it" was going to be hers even if she got "it" with borrowed money.

This exchange made me reflect on my own "its" that I just had to have or still might be yearning for. Was I willing to sacrifice and make my life more complicated because I was not satisfied with what I had? Did I rush into certain relationships, career moves and positions prematurely instead of waiting on God to tell me to move? Was it possible I was in a secret competition with others and decided to purchase items and things to keep up a perceived image and lifestyle? When things were going wrong in my life and all hell was breaking loose, did I try to solve my own issues surrounding myself with "more." Of course I did. And so did you.

It is time for us to shake this notion that we must have more in order to be happy and to have joy. We are swayed with glitz and glamour and shiny things and with others' possessions. The world has persuaded us to believe that without these things, we cannot live a life full of abundance. We continue to want more and more and more, and we are never satisfied. Now, having things and prestige is not all bad and mean you are not living a great and blessed life. However, we must all be careful not to strive so hard to obtain all of these worldly things that will mean nothing in the end.

I want to be satisfied. I am going into 2018 with the mindset that I will thank and praise God for what He has given me today. If he sees fit for me to receive more and bless me with more, I will praise Him for his blessings. However, if God decides that what I have is enough, I will continue to praise and bless His name for my enough. God wins in 2018 when we recognize that what He provides is enough, and we can be satisfied. Paul reminds us – "Not that I am speaking of being in need, for I have learned in whatever situation I am to be content." Be content. You will win.

God Wins...
It's Ok to Be Happy

I know that there is nothing better for people than to be happy and to do good while they live. Ecclesiastes 3:12

Ok. Ok. Ok. I admit I am a complainer. I cannot help it, I suppose. I grew up in a house with grandparents who complained about everything. Complaining is in my DNA. I admittedly may be a complainer, but I am also someone who tends to do something for the very thing or person I am complaining about. I have learned that complaining just to complain with no actions solves absolutely nothing and only leaves you with heartburn.

However, what I have observed over time is that people who complain about this or that are absolutely miserable. They are always upset or disturbed by something. They get irritated when you speak to them but will talk about you like a dog when you forget to say good morning that one time. You tell them how beautiful the weather is outside, and they reply with yesterday's sun was brighter. These are the people you cannot share your excitement and good news with because they will find at least one negative thing to say to you to bring your spirits down and dull your shine. These people are unhappy, and are living in misery.

I understand life for so many just plain ole sucks right now. The world around us is dark and leaves little light for hope. Marriages are struggling and strained. Husbands and wives live almost separate lives while residing under the same roof. He does his thing and she does her thing, and they only come together when they must. The happiness and bliss they both thought they would encounter as a union went skipping out the door holding hands immediately after the couple returned from the honeymoon. Not married? Well the relationship goals you want to emulate from social media are not quite coming together as planned. You are ready to settle down, but your partner still has that wandering eye and spirit. You are holding on hoping that he or she will see that you are the only one that can make them truly happy in life. What about your job/career? Yup. At work things are all just a hot mess! I get it. Trust me, I do. All around you and me things are heavy and burdensome. It is a lot to take in and to handle, and we can only take but so much.

Yes, I get it. But what about when things are going right? What about when there is really no reason to complain or be unhappy? Your marriage might not be perfect, but there is love there and you know for sure you could not live life without your spouse. Your boss might be crazy and out of control, but you work with the best group of co-workers on this side of glory, and they make coming to work easier to do. What about the fact that you have more than what you had last year. The more may not be over the top but it is more than you had before. Here is what I am trying to show you – we do not know how to be happy even when there are plenty things to be happy about.

Negativity and pessimism drive us. We almost cannot function unless there is a problem. We enjoy playing in the mud instead of soaring in the sky. We pitch our tents in the depths of darkness and we say we want to come up for air and light, but when the light shines we complain it is too bright. We find at least one problem with everything and everyone, and we are not satisfied until we enlarge the one minor problem. We see absolutely no positive, and that must immediately end.

This year I found these words marching out of my mouth more often than not when engaging with people – "It is ok to be happy!" Yup. Just that simple. You don't need a special celebration or party to be happy. Everything in life does not have to be going as you have perfectly planned it in your mind. You do not have to create chaos and look with a magnifying glass to find the one thing to complain about so you can exclaim, "See, I told you it was too good to be true!" You do not have to be "that" person at work and in staff meetings. And you know what I mean by "that" person. You can be happy and find the good and joy that surrounds you daily but is missed because of the blinders of negativity.

Ok. I am not saying be naïve and unrealistic. Yes, there are times when you must deal with the "bad." Life is not perfect. What I am saying is handle it, then move on. Stop creating drama and mess that does not exist so that you can function. If things are going well, enjoy them and live in the good times. Relax. Smile.

2018 can be your opportunity to come out from the shadows of negativity. You can do it. I give you permission. It is ok to be happy. Yes, God will win in 2018 when we shed negativity for there is nothing better for people than to be happy and to do good while they live. Do you accept the challenge?

God
Wins... Mistakes

For the sake of Christ, then, I am content with weaknesses, insults, hardships, persecutions, and calamities. For when I am weak, then I am strong. 2 Corinthians 12:10

I am afraid to mess up. I am my biggest critic and harder on myself than anyone else on this planet. I hate letting people down. I am unrealistic with my own expectations and the perceived expectations of others for me. I cannot mess up; things must be perfect if my hands have touched them. Unrealistic. I know. Yet, I struggle with making mistakes. And although I have become slightly more comfortable with the fact that every day I wake up I am guaranteed to make a mistake and I do not walk on water, my stress level peaks at times with just the thought of making a mistake.

I am not sure how I became so fearful of making mistakes and letting people down. Perhaps, once again, words, experiences, and interactions from my childhood have helped to create the warped thought processes of my mind. Perhaps it is because no matter what I did to try to please my grandmother, I came up short and would always make mistakes. Or perhaps it is because my grandfather told me I was not worthy of gifts and special privileges because I made too many mistakes including having my child. Perhaps it is because family members alluded to the fact that I was the mistake that pushed my mother into the grip of alcohol and drugs. Perhaps?

I understand that to whom much is given much is required, and I am always ready and on point to tackle any challenge. I have been given much responsibility. And

I accept it. However, I decided to sit back in 2017 and analyze and even take notes. Yes, I took literal notes on how people view me and the things I do. One major thing stuck out to me – people, including my inner circle, rarely expect me to make mistakes, and when I do, hell freezes over and the world stops. "What?" "She messed up?" "The perfect one got it wrong?" "Hmmm, she tried it... and failed!" I am shown no mercy. Or at least I feel like that is the case. Perhaps I have created this facade of perfection which leaves the door wide open for people to judge my slipups. I need to be realistic about myself and my stumbles. So do you.

Well, we all make mistakes. Day after day we make mistakes whether big or small. We make mistakes. Some of us are able to recognize the mistakes we make while some of us takes a little longer. Some of us vow to never make the same mistakes again while others of us relive our mistakes like Groundhog Day. We have made mistakes that have left permeant scars and damage, and we can never fully recover. We also have made mistakes where we must learn to forgive ourselves even when others cannot forgive us. We are only human - flesh – born to make mistakes. Mistakes are inevitable.

I am flawed. I admit and recognize this truth, and I am becoming more comfortable with my flaws and faults. What about you? When we fully accept that we are weak and our mistakes are due to our human limitations that is when God can be made perfect. For the sake of Christ, then, I am content with weaknesses, insults, hardships, persecutions, and calamities. For when I am weak, then I am strong. God wins in 2018, yes, even through our mistakes. His grace is sufficient.

God Wins...

His Promises

For I know the plans I have for you," declares the Lord, "plans to prosper you and not to harm you, plans to give you hope and a future. Jeremiah 29:11

Discouraged. Confused. Irritated. Unsure. Numb. I listened to these descriptors come out of the mouth of one of the few women I highly regard. Once again, 2017 hit. This time someone I loved deeply was experiencing a type of hurt that ripped her heart wide open and there was absolutely nothing I could do but to sit back and listen. I am a fixer. I wanted so desperately to fix this problem for her and make the pain go away – but I could not. "I think God has forgotten about me." She said. "He is too silent. What about the promises He made?" We cried and as the tears fell, I whispered, "please show up now Lord."

He didn't. Well, at least he did not show up in the form and fashion we both wanted him to show up. We wanted Him to erase the entire situation out of existence as if it never happened. He is God right? He is in control of everything, and that includes time, right? Then He could go back in time and prevent all of this from happening in the first place, and my loved one would be just fine. But God does not operate in that manner. He does not answer to man or woman. He is God. He moves in His time, and it is always the right time.

To date, God has not moved in my loved one's particular crisis. Yet I know without a shadow of a doubt, He will. See God is not a man he should lie. He will keep His promises. His word is true. He is unlike my mother who made promises to me as a child and each time I would believe her, yet over and over again she broke her promises to me. We never did make it to the playground together. Or take that walk. Promises are meant to be kept and not to be broken.

God made me a promise the evening of January 10, 1996. My grandmother, the woman who for me at the age of 17, I truly felt was immortal, had been scheduled for her second heart bypass surgery. I could tell she was nervous leading up to the scheduled date, but she was strong and, of course, she would be just fine – I thought to myself. Well, the blizzard of 1996 wreaked havoc on our city, and everything was at a complete standstill. That meant my grandmother's surgery had to be postponed. Her heart could not wait, and exactly one day after the scheduled surgery, date she was in tremendous pain, and we called for an ambulance. Our street was covered completely by the snow. The ambulance had no way possible to get down our street. So they sent fire fighters in to retrieve my grandmother. I watched in despair as the fire fighters maneuvered and made a way to exit my grandmother out of the house, up the street, and into the waiting ambulance. I remember how she looked at me; and I was terrified. I had never ever witnessed a look of alarm in her eyes all of my life. She was afraid. My superhero was afraid. That moment is forever etched in my mind.

She made it to the hospital, and the next day our street was cleared and I went to visit her. She was sitting up and talking while I visited. I did not stay long, and told her I would be back the next day to visit her again. She looked fine. I was worried for no reason at all. Her super powers had returned and I would see her the next day.

That early evening the phone rang. Pop answered, had a brief conversation, and then hung up the phone. "I need to call all of the family." He said to me. "Why?" I inquired. "Stop asking all of these questions," he sternly rebuked me. "Stay here with the baby; I am going to the hospital." He left. Something was wrong. I knew something was wrong. Why would all of the family need to go to the hospital? Why? Then it hit me! Naw. No way. God would not call my grandmother home. No way. My mother had just died three months ago; there is no way He would do this to me.

I sunk into the couch. My mind was racing and my heart was fluttering. And then He spoke as if he was sitting right next to me. "I need to take your grandmother, but you and the baby will be alright." NOOOOOOO! I screamed. The person in the room looked at me as if I was crazy. He was not privy to the message God had just delivered to me. I sat in astonishment. Tense. Waiting.

Thirty minutes later the phone rang and I was upstairs. All I heard was "she's gone." The rest was a blur. I have no clue how I made it down the steps or how I opened the door for my next door neighbors who heard me screaming and crying through the walls, and I was so loud they thought someone was in the house trying to hurt me. I collapsed at the front door. "What's wrong?" "What's wrong?" they said as they attempted to lift me up off the ground. "My grandmother is dead," I told them.

My life from that moment on has never been the same. I miss her with all of my heart and my soul. She was my rock; my everything. She was my consistency in life. My lifeline. How would I make it without her? It did not seem like it could even be possible. Who would I be without her? Unfair. Yes, perhaps, unfair.

But God. He has blessed my life beyond my wildest dreams and imagination. Even when everything points to destruction all around me God finds a way to work it all out in my favor. He has made ways out of no way for me time and time again. I often ask, "Why God? Why do you continue to do all of this for me especially when I continually fall short of your word and expectations?" And He gently reminds me of His promise made to me in that beginning month of the year in 1996. I am standing on God's promises; and He always comes through on His word.

God says, "for I know for I know the plans I have for you; plans to prosper you and not to harm you, plans to give you hope and a future. He is a promise keeper and even when He has not responded yet in our particular situation, He is there, and He will show up right on time. God wins in 2018 when we remember His promises. My God! My God! I praise you for the best is yet to come!

God Wins...
Refresh and Restore

"He restores my soul. He leads me in paths of righteousness for his name's sake." Psalm 23:3

Burned out. I am burned out. I am beyond exhausted. My cup is not half full it is bone dry. The fumes I was running on have evaporated – gone. I have nothing left to give. 2017 has wiped me out. Again, the truth of the matter is 2017 was not that bad of a year for me in terms of overall life circumstances. Things were pretty good. Yet, and in spite of, I am on 'E.'

My energy engine will not start. I keep turning the key and pumping the gas petal, but it keeps turning over and I go nowhere. I feel pathetic. Limp. Hopeless maybe. Just plain old tired and worn down. Thirsty and in need of nourishment and fulfillment. Something to change to motivate me to keep on keeping on. 2017 has made it evident to me that no matter what I try to do to get myself together and to push forward to do more and more, I will continue to fail without some sort of change. But what is that change?

I am involved in a lot of things in my life. I am active in my church and organizations. I sit on boards, work in the community, have a demanding career; and a family. People always say to me that I am so busy, and, yes I admit my schedule is usually blocked and filled from 5:30 a.m. – 9:00 p.m. every day. Yet, I always have this sense that I am not doing enough and actually should be doing more. I shared this thought with my sister friend, and she said, "You are nuts!" How can you possibly put anything else on your plate? Yeah. I guess she is right – gluttony is a sin – right?

Whenever my phone rings, a text comes through, or an email pops up on my screen 9.5 times out of 10, it is someone asking me some sort of question or to do something for them. It is a very rare occasion the messages I receive ask me how I am doing or if I need help with anything. Of course, I feel this obligation that I must handle all requests received. I almost take on this kind of responsibility for everyone else's personal welfare. I have to help them and do for them because ...well, I am needed...right? People have come to expect this responsive behavior from me. They know, I know, I cannot let them down and will take care of it without a shadow of a doubt. They recognize that I will continue to do for them with no expectation of a return. Frankly, I cannot blame them totally for taking and rarely ever giving. I have allowed them to use me for their gain at my own personal expense. It is my fault. I never drew a line in the sand – no boundaries were set. And hence the reason I now look in the mirror and wonder why the bags on my eyes hang so low –where did they come from?

I am being pulled in multiple directions – people are pulling on my legs, my arms, my side and some even try to pull me by my weave. Enough is enough! Self-check! I am only one individual and cannot be and do it all...right? Something has to change. But wait! I prayed over and over again to God that He would bless me so that I can be a blessing. If I do not help others, then my prayers were in vain. And then, of course, God speaks and tells me I cannot give what I do not have. How can I possibly continue to pour into others when my vessel is empty? I become more of a hindrance to others instead of a blessing.

It is time for me to refresh and restore. I have lost my joy in helping others, and it has now become an obligation. My anxiety level actually rises every time my phone chimes because I am anticipating another request of me, and honestly, I do not want to do it. I do not feel like solving the problem. Want to know a little secret... I actually get angry at the person. That is not good at all... I know.

Time for a major change in my life. I do not want to resent people for doing to me what I have allowed them to do. I honestly have a heart and desire to help others. That is one of my purposes in life, and I know that for certain. But how can I be there for others when they need me and fill my tank at the same time? How do I create a balance?

I want a willing spirit. Therefore, I must refresh and restore. It has to be mandatory in my life I take true time for me: praying, meditating, soaking in the beauty of this world; unplugging from the noise. I must be intentional about scheduling consistent times just for me, and I have to believe that that is ok to do. In fact, it is absolutely a necessity for me to do or else I will remain empty.

Are you like me by chance? Do you give and give and give and feel like no one understands or appreciates ALL that you do? Are you running low and need to be filled up and re-energized? Are you ready to be willing to help again because it is the desire of your heart? Well, God wins in 2018 if we take time to refresh and restore and realize that we are not being selfish we are preserving our lives. God will restore to you the joy of His salvation, and uphold you with a willing spirit. Relax and rest and then sit back and watch how God fills you up to continue the great work.

God

Wins... Health

Do you not know that your bodies are temples of the Holy Spirit, who is in you, whom you have received from God? You are not your own; you were bought at a price. Therefore honor God with your bodies. Corinthians 6:19-20

Thump! My husband said it sounded like a large sack of potatoes had hit the ground. All I remember is looking up at paramedics looking down at me and working on me. I told them I was ok and would call the doctor the next day and there was no need to go to the hospital. They took me anyhow, and I was admitted. The next day, I was tested for heart problems. I left the hospital on three new medicines. Unfortunately, that would not be my last hospital visit or stay. Over the next several years, I was in and out of the emergency room and hospital with one aliment or another, things I had never even heard of and some symptoms the doctors have yet to figure out. At the age of 34, I was carrying around an entire plastic zip-lock storage bag in my purse filled with prescription medicines. Sad. How did I get here?

I gained over 50 pounds and looked and felt a mess. No matter what I tried to do, my weight continued to balloon up and so did my depression level. My health was suffering, but I did not know what to do. I knew I was no longer extremely attractive or appealing to my husband because I was not alluring to myself. I was sick all of the time, 24 hours a day, 7 days a week. I prayed and nothing happened. I prayed and nothing happened. I prayed and nothing happened.

Then I prayed and I took some action. Once again after a conversation with a friend, the answers I was searching for hit ME like a sack of potatoes. If I wanted to be healthy again, I must change my lifestyle. I had to comprehend that what I eat and drink and how I take care of my body must honesty be a lifestyle change and not a fad for the moment kind of thing. It would be hard to do but not impossible. I witnessed many of others around me make it happen in their lives so why not me too?

Intentionally adopting a healthier lifestyle is hard for me because I have to erase years of unhealthy habits. See, my grandparents and family are from the south – Mississippi to be exact. So I grew up on butter cakes, hammocks, chitterlings, fried fish and chicken, and do not forget the baked macaroni and cheese. Mmmm. Mmmm. Good. Delicious! My mouth is watering from just thinking about the food. These foods are not bad for me every once in a while if eaten in moderation; my problem is that I sometimes ate them for breakfast, snack, lunch, dinner, and snack again. And then I had the nerve to say, "I don't know why I keep gaining weight? It must be these medicines." Whoa!!!

And let's not even begin to start on exercising. Growing up absolutely no grown person in my family moved a finger let alone their bodies to exercise. I thought that since I was an athlete and active as a young person, I would forever have that body no matter what I ate and what extremity I did not move. Boy was I upside down and wrong all the way around. It all caught up to me and I was suffering.

I made a lifestyle change because I realized how much I wanted to live for myself and for my family and friends. I had too many health scares. And although I am still faced with unanswered health concerns even today, I am much better off now than I have been in a very long time. Now, I have much more work to do, but I am certainly on my way. My health and my outlook on being healthy have greatly improved. My body is a temple.

My friends, put down the greasy hamburger and supersized fries every day, and put on your running shoes and take that walk. In 2018 God wins when we make our health a priority and make those much needed lifestyle changes. Be reminded that our bodies are temples of the Holy Spirit, who is in us, whom we have received from God? We are not our own; and were brought at a price. Therefore, we must honor God with our bodies. This a commandment – not optional.

God Wins...

Be Strong and Do The Work

Be strong and courageous, and do the work. Do not be afraid or discouraged, for the LORD God, my God, is with you. He will not fail you or forsake you until all the work for the service of the temple of the LORD is finished. 1 Chronicles 28:20

"Let *me tell you something you already know. The world ain't all sunshine and rainbows. It is a very mean and nasty place, and I don't care how tough you are, it will beat you to your knees and keep you there permanently if you let it. You, me or nobody is gonna hit as hard as life. But it ain't about how hard you hit; it's about how hard you can get hit and keep moving forward.. It's how much you can take, and keep moving forward. That's how winning is done . Now, if you know what you're worth, then go out and get what you're worth. But you gotta be willing to take the hits and not point fingers and blame other people. Cowards do that, and that ain't you. You're better than that!*"

This is one of my favorite scenes and speeches from my favorite movie series of all time – <u>Rocky Balboa</u>. Those who know me, I mean really know me, know that I am obsessed with <u>Rocky</u> movies. If I happened to stumble across a <u>Rocky</u> marathon on t.v., I must stop everything I am doing and watch from start to finish. I own the entire collection. I watch the movie <u>Creed</u> at least one time every weekend. I am addicted. I know. But I am not apologetic. Rocky movies go way beyond the thrill of the fight for me; they are jammed pack with inspirational life lessons that remind me that no matter what I am facing, if I am willing to put in the work and fight hard, I can be a winner.

In this particular scene, Rocky is talking to his son about life knocking him down and the fact that we have to make decisions on whether or not we will get back up and keep moving forward. "WE" have to make those choices; not our mothers, fathers, sisters, friends...no one else but the man or woman we look at in the mirror day after day. That is hard work. It requires suffering. It is no easy feat. It is going to be painful.

Winners push through the pain. They see the benefits of "going through" because ultimately there is victory on the other side of through. Too many times individuals cry, moan, and complain about all of their hardships and big shadows. It is everyone else's responsibility and fault as to why this or that happened in our lives and why we cannot get ahead. And even when others have indeed contributed to our issues, we fail to admit to ourselves that we share some responsibility, and we ultimately can make a change. We point fingers. We take the punches, get knocked down, and wait for the referee to save us by the count.

I met with a group of young women who are recent college graduates. Each of the young women is intelligent, beautiful, talented, and has what it takes to be a winner. As I listened to them describe to me their future hopes and aspirations and why they felt they were not where they wanted to be in life, I could not help but say to myself, "Wow these young ladies are lost." They have everything and every opportunity they could possibly imagine at their feet but refuse to see the tree of life through the forest. To them, everyone else has made their life journey and career paths so difficult to maneuver. I was met with a barrage of "if - then" statements; all, of course, went like "if my parents would only give me a few more months living rent free, then I would be able to save more money and move out and get my own place." They failed to admit they have been living rent free for almost five years in their parent's basement, and, to date, they saved a whopping total of $150.

The microwave, do-it-for-me, society is killing us all. We want it all, and we want it all right now. But we do not want to earn it, pay for it, put our blood, sweat and tears into it - no way! Why would we actually work for want we want in life? I should be able to upload my video and sit back and watch my success "appear" through likes, shares, and views. That mentality is just absurd.

Well that might sound a little harsh, but the reality is people are becoming allergic to hard work. Hard work brings about good results...even if the results are not immediate. I believe in 2017 I took my eyes off the prize of life. I started looking out the side window view and refused to face it all head on. I allowed our new societal norms to overrule my natural instincts of being strong, courageous and hardworking and failed to finish what I started.

Perhaps 2017 has been stagnate for you because you forgot the importance and the necessity of hard work. Instead, you pointed your fingers and blamed everything and everyone else including the personification of the year 2017 itself. Yup. It is 2017's fault we became lazy and lacked drive and motivation. Yeah right. So here's the challenge – are you going to stay knocked down or will you get up? I ain't hear no bell; we got one more round! God wins in 2018 - be strong and courageous and do the work.

God
Wins...
Trust Him

May the God of hope fill you with all joy and peace as you trust in him, so that you may overflow with hope by the power of the Holy Spirit. Romans 15:13

Well, we made it! I hope you enjoyed the journey as much as I have and have learned as much as I have learned. Bottom line is life is something else no matter what year it is. Things will continue to go haywire, and we will be met with obstacle after obstacle. There will be dark days and pitch black nights. We are going to cry. We are going to cry a lot. People are going to continue to hurt us intentionally and unintentionally. Death and destruction will not go away on this side of glory. Abuse, neglect, loneliness, and despair will still peak their heads into our lives. Life on this earth will continue to go on.

It is going to be rough. Not all things we try to accomplish will be easy. We will be misunderstood and taken the wrong way. We will be overlooked and overshadowed. We will be overly exhausted. We will experienced trying times with our finances and our health and perhaps all at the same time. Our businesses will fail before they succeed. Our children will disappoint us, and our spouses or significant others will fail our expectations. We will feel we are walking alone and that we are being beat up on every side. We will be pulled in a myriad of different directions, and we will be picking up and carrying heavy loads. We will make mistakes, forget about our hopes and dreams, and fail to forgive others and ourselves. We will spill the tea just a little and temporarily put back on the mask. We will be human.

In 2018 life will continue. Without a shadow of a doubt, unless the good Lord calls us home, life for us all will move forward with all of the good and the bad. The questions then become for us: How will we manage and handle it all while we are in the midst of it all? What will be our plan? Will we depend on our own strength, power, and limited authority? Will we take matters into our own hands and wish for the best? Will we stay knocked down? Or will we take on 2018 the way God desires us to in order to win and live our best life- and that is to Trust HIM.

I can tell you without hesitation or reservation I know what I plan to do. I am going to trust in the Lord with ALL my heart and lean not to my own understanding. I will submit to him, and His word promises me that he will direct my paths. Lord, when I am afraid, I will put my trust in you. I fully acknowledge that when I choose to trust in myself, I am a fool, but when I trust in the Lord, I walk in wisdom and will be kept safe. I will let not my heart be troubled. I believe in God. And he who is sitting on the throne of Grace is making everything new and his words are trustworthy and true.

Hallelujah! We win because God already has the victory! We no longer have to be stuck in the mud of hopelessness and the "what if's." It is so because God said so. Spoiler alert – when we get to the end of the story

– God Wins! And those of us who trust and believe in Him win as well. So we do not have to fret or worry. Be encouraged. God will not only win in 2018; He also wins forever and ever. Trust in Him, and may the God of hope fill you with all joy and peace as you trust in him, so that you may overflow with hope by the power of the Holy Spirit.

Be Blessed.

Made in the USA
Columbia, SC
07 February 2018